LeBRON JAMES

Awesome Athletes

Jameson Anderson

Checkerboard Library

An Imprint of Abdo Publishing
www.abdopublishing.com

www.abdopublishing.com

Published by Abdo Publishing, a division of ABDO, PO Box 398166, Minneapolis, Minnesota 55439. Copyright © 2015 by Abdo Consulting Group, Inc. International copyrights reserved in all countries. No part of this book may be reproduced in any form without written permission from the publisher. Checkerboard Library™ is a trademark and logo of Abdo Publishing.

Printed in the United States of America, North Mankato, Minnesota.
052014
092014

THIS BOOK CONTAINS
RECYCLED MATERIALS

Cover Photo: AP Images
Interior Photos: Alamy p. 7; AP Images pp. 1, 5, 9, 11, 13, 15, 17, 19, 20, 21, 23, 24, 25, 27, 29

Series Coordinator: Tamara L. Britton
Editors: Rochelle Baltzer, Bridget O'Brien
Art Direction: Neil Klinepier

Library of Congress Cataloging-in-Publication Data

Anderson, Jameson.
  Lebron James / Jameson Anderson.
     pages cm. -- (Awesome athletes)
  Includes index.
  ISBN 978-1-62403-330-8
1. James, LeBron--Juvenile literature. 2. Basketball players--United States--Biography--Juvenile literature. I. Title.
  GV884.J36A64 2015
  796.323092--dc23
  [B]
                                2014000176

TABLE OF CONTENTS

ANOTHER RECORD

On January 16, 2013, the Miami Heat took on the Golden State Warriors. It could have been an ordinary game. But LeBron James was about to make history at Oracle Arena in Oakland, California.

Late in the second quarter, James made a shot that put him in the record books. He became the youngest player ever to score 20,000 career points. Once again, James's name and age were a topic on all the sports shows.

James was already the youngest player ever **drafted**. He was the youngest to be named **Rookie** of the Year. James was also the youngest to score both 1,000 and 10,000 points in his career. Now, he was the youngest to score 20,000 points.

The Heat defeated the Warriors 92–75 that night. James and his teammates had won the **National Basketball Association (NBA)** Finals the previous year. With this win, they were on their way to a second championship!

LeBron James scored 25 points and had 7 rebounds and 10 assists on the way to scoring his 20,000th point.

HIGHLIGHT REEL

LeBron Raymone James was born in Akron, Ohio.

1984

James became the youngest player to be named Rookie of the Year.

2004

The Heat defeated the Oklahoma City Thunder 4–1 for the NBA Championship; James was named the NBA Finals Most Valuable Player.

2012

The Heat lost to the San Antonio Spurs 4–1 in the NBA Finals.

2014

2003

The Cleveland Cavaliers made James the number one pick in the NBA Draft.

2010

Dwyane Wade, Chris Bosh, and James signed with the Miami Heat.

2013

The Heat defeated the San Antonio Spurs 4–3 for their second NBA Championship; James won his second Finals MVP award.

LEBRON JAMES

DOB: December 30, 1984
Ht: 6'8"
Wt: 250
Position: Forward
Number: 6
Shoots: Right

CAREER AVERAGES:
Assists Per Game:	6.9
Rebounds Per Game:	7.2
Points Per Game:	27.5

AWARDS:
All-Star Game MVP: 2006, 2008
NBA Champion: 2012, 2013
NBA Finals MVP: 2012, 2013
NBA MVP: 2009, 2010, 2012, 2013
NBA Scoring Champion: 2008
Rookie of the Year: 2004

ROUGH BEGINNING

LeBron Raymone James was born in Akron, Ohio, on December 30, 1984. LeBron's mother, Gloria, was just 16 years old when he was born. The two lived in a tiny house with LeBron's grandmother, great-grandmother, and two uncles. The whole family helped take care of LeBron.

LeBron's great-grandmother died when he was an infant. Just three years later, on Christmas day, his grandmother died of a heart attack.

Gloria didn't have a steady job. Without the support of LeBron's grandmothers, she struggled to pay the bills. The house was old and in need of repairs. Gloria couldn't afford to pay for heat.

LeBron and his mom soon moved in with a neighbor. After that, they stayed with friends. Without a job, LeBron's mother moved them around a lot. They often slept on couches in friends' apartments.

LeBron's mother called her son "Bron Bron."

TROUBLE WITH SCHOOL

In 1993, LeBron and his mother moved five times in three months. When LeBron was in fourth grade, his mother was often busy and left LeBron alone. Many days, he chose not to go to school. He missed nearly 100 days!

It seemed as if LeBron's life would be difficult for a long time. But in the summer of 1993, LeBron's life began to change. A youth football coach named Bruce Kelker saw him playing tag with other kids.

Coach Kelker challenged the boys to a footrace. Whoever could run across the parking lot the fastest would be his football team's running back. LeBron came in first. He won by 15 yards (14 m)!

Coach Kelker asked LeBron if he wanted to join a football team. LeBron was just nine years old. He had never played organized youth sports. But LeBron said yes.

Today, LeBron enjoys meeting his young fans and teaching them about the importance of education.

TEAM MOTHER

Coach Kelker would become an important man in LeBron's life. LeBron's mother couldn't afford to pay for football equipment. So, Coach Kelker paid the bill. He also picked up LeBron and took him to practice. Then, the coach drove LeBron back to where he was staying.

Eventually, LeBron and his mother moved in with Coach Kelker. LeBron's mother helped with cooking and contributed money for bills. She became a "team mother" and helped organize the team's practices.

LeBron had finally found stability in his life. Soon he became the star of the team. He played running back and scored 17 touchdowns his first season.

No matter what age he is or what sport he plays, LeBron's mother loves to cheer for her son.

LEARNING A NEW SPORT

Coach Kelker's home soon became too crowded. So, LeBron went to live with another coach, Frank Walker, and his wife, Pam. LeBron's mother moved in with friends. She still went to LeBron's games. She also spent time with him on weekends.

When football season ended, Coach Walker had a new sport for LeBron to try. LeBron learned to play basketball.

An even bigger change happened when the Walkers **enrolled** LeBron at Portage Path Elementary School. There, LeBron found that art, music, and gym were his favorite classes.

Coach Walker and his wife helped LeBron with his schoolwork. They made him do homework after school before he could practice basketball. LeBron liked school so much that he didn't miss another class all year. At the end of fifth grade, LeBron won his school's attendance award.

LeBron learned how to play a better game with lots of practice, and by coaching a basketball team for eight-year-olds when he was nine. By the time he was in high school, LeBron could easily think his way around the court.

HIGH SCHOOL BALL

Soon, LeBron's basketball skills were gaining attention around the country. In 1997, his team qualified for a national tournament. In eighth grade, the team went all the way to the championship game. But they lost to a team from southern California 68–66.

Now, LeBron had to choose a high school. He and his friends wanted to keep playing together. So, they all **enrolled** at Saint Vincent-Saint Mary High School in Akron. There, they would play for the Fighting Irish.

LeBron was a starter on the **varsity** team as a freshman. He wore No. 23 in honor of his favorite **NBA** player, Michael Jordan. The Fighting Irish finished with a perfect record that year. And, they won the state championship. LeBron averaged 18 points per game, but he scored 25 in the championship game!

NICKNAME

WHEN LEBRON WAS IN TENTH GRADE, A NEWSPAPER REPORTER NICKNAMED HIM "KING JAMES." THE NAME HAS STUCK WITH HIM THROUGH HIS NBA DAYS.

By the time LeBron was in tenth grade, his high school had to hold home games at the University of Akron. So many people wanted to see LeBron play that the high school wouldn't hold them all!

People from the Akron area weren't the only ones who wanted to see LeBron play. College and **NBA** coaches and **scouts** were also interested in following him.

LeBron celebrates after the Fighting Irish win 65–45 against Virginia's Oak Hill Academy.

COLLEGE OR NBA?

LeBron did well in high school and maintained a B average. He likely could have earned a basketball **scholarship** and chosen almost any college he wanted.

Yet, LeBron knew that he could also go on to the **NBA**. As he entered his senior year, the choice became clear. He would declare himself eligible for the NBA **Draft**.

The Cleveland Cavaliers were a local team. As the season approached, they hoped to draft LeBron. They wanted to build a better team around him. Many other teams hoped to have the first pick in the draft in order to sign LeBron.

Dreams came true for LeBron and Cleveland fans. The Cavaliers drafted LeBron with the first overall pick in the 2003 NBA Draft. He signed a three-year contract for $12.96 million.

FUN FACT

IN HIS TIME AT SAINT VINCENT-SAINT MARY HIGH SCHOOL, LEBRON SCORED 2,657 POINTS AND HAD 892 REBOUNDS AND 523 ASSISTS.

As the 2003 NBA Draft approached, it became known as the "LeBron Lottery." The Cleveland Cavaliers were able to snag LeBron with the draft's first pick.

James spent the first seven years of his career with the Cleveland Cavaliers. He made a name for himself on and off the court. He was loved by fans around the world.

During his first season with the Cavaliers, James became the third **rookie** to average 20 points per game. The first two were Oscar Robertson and Michael Jordan.

James continued to make history. At the end of the 2003–2004 season, he became the youngest player to win Rookie of the Year. He also became

James became the youngest player to score a triple-double when he scored 27 points and had 11 rebounds and 10 assists against the Portland Trail Blazers.

the youngest player to score more than 40 points in a single game. And at 20 years old, James became the youngest player to score a **triple-double** during his second **NBA** season.

In the 2005–2006 season, James led the Cavaliers to the **playoffs**. They lost in the second round, but James had proven that he was an NBA superstar.

In 2004, James was presented with the Rookie of the Year award.

The Cavaliers signed James to a contract extension. He received $60 million to play another three years.

OFF THE COURT

Companies also loved James. They wanted him to advertise their products. James has made millions through product **endorsements**. Nike, McDonald's, Samsung, and State Farm have paid James to advertise for them.

James shares his success with his community. In 2004, he started the LeBron James Family Foundation. This group helps kids do better in school, stay physically active, and care for the **environment**.

The foundation also helps single-parent families. James remembers his own struggles growing up. He wants other kids growing up in Akron to have strong family connections. James works with groups such as the Boys and Girls Clubs as well.

James also makes TV appearances. He has hosted both the ESPY Awards on ESPN and the variety show *Saturday Night Live*.

The LeBron James Family Foundation hosts bike-a-thons for kids.
James likes to ride with them.

James has grown into a strong father himself. He married his high school sweetheart, Savannah Brinson, on September 14, 2013. They have two sons, LeBron Jr. and Bryce Maximus.

OLYMPIC MEDALS

In his **rookie** season in the **NBA**, James was selected for the US Olympic basketball team. He played at the 2004 Summer Olympics in Athens, Greece. The US team came home with a bronze medal.

James scores against Spain in the 2012 gold medal game.

In 2012, James celebrated with Kevin Durant, Carmelo Anthony, and Kobe Bryant (*left to right*) after winning their gold medals.

James's Olympic career didn't end there. He returned with the US team to the 2008 Summer Olympics in Beijing, China. James loved playing with **NBA** stars such as Dwyane Wade, Chris Bosh, and Carmelo Anthony. The team won gold against Spain in the final round.

Team USA returned to the Olympic court in 2012 in London, England. Once again, James helped the team bring home the gold.

LEAVING CLEVELAND

The 2010 season didn't end well for James and the Cavaliers. While they made the **playoffs**, James scored just 15 points in Game 5 of the second round against the Boston Celtics. Cleveland fans booed when James left the court.

James was an unrestricted free agent after the season. This meant he could go to any team he wanted to. Many teams wanted to sign James.

ESPN worked with James to make the announcement of his choice on TV. Just days before the announcement, James's friends Dwyane Wade and Chris Bosh signed with the Miami Heat.

When James announced to the world that he would play for the Heat, he received a lot of criticism. Some fans thought he should stay in Cleveland. The team's owner, Dan Gilbert, wrote a letter expressing his anger over James's decision. He thought James was showing off by making an appearance on a TV show. The criticism didn't matter to James. He stayed focused on his goals.

James (*left*) enjoyed playing basketball with Bosh (*middle*) and Wade (*right*) during the Olympics. He was excited to play on the same team again when he signed with the Heat.

THE CHAMPION

In his second season with the Heat, James did what he could not do in Cleveland. In 2012, the team finished 46–20 and defeated the Boston Celtics for the conference title. The Oklahoma City Thunder waited in the **NBA** Finals. The Heat won the championship 4–1. During Game 5, James scored a **triple-double**, with 26 points, 13 assists, and 11 **rebounds**. He was named the MVP.

The next year, the Heat improved to 66–16. They beat the Indiana Pacers to again win their conference. In the Finals, they defeated the San Antonio Spurs 4–3. James scored triple-doubles in Games 1 and 6. He was the second player to score two triple-doubles in the same Finals series since Magic Johnson in 1991. He was again named MVP.

In 2014, the 54–28 Heat once again won their conference, defeating the Indiana Pacers. The team became just the third in history to reach the Finals four years in a row.

James dunks for two of his 31 points in Game 5 of the 2014 Finals. The Spurs took the game 104–87 to win the NBA Championship.

The Heat once again met the Spurs. The Heat lost Game 1. In Game 2, James scored 35 points and had 10 **rebounds**.

In the fourth quarter, Miami was down by one point. James passed the ball to Bosh. Bosh scored a three-pointer! The Heat won 98–96. It was their only victory. On June 15, the Spurs won the series 4–1.

On July 1, 2014, James became an unrestricted free agent. On July 12, he signed a two-year, $42.1 million contract with the Cleveland Cavaliers. James said he would finish his career in his home state. He wants to deliver Cleveland's first sports championship in 50 years. If anyone can do it, LeBron James can!

GLOSSARY

draft - an event during which sports teams choose new players. Choosing new players is known as drafting them.

endorsement - the act of publicly recommending a product or service in exchange for money.

enroll - to register, especially in order to attend school.

environment - all the surroundings that affect the growth and well-being of a living thing.

National Basketball Association (NBA) - a professional basketball league in the United States and Canada. It consists of an Eastern and a Western conference, each with three divisions. There are 30 teams in the NBA.

playoffs - a series of games that determine which team will win a championship.

rebound - the act of gaining control of the basketball after a missed shot.

rookie - a first-year player in a professional sport.

scholarship - money or aid given to help a student continue his or her studies.

scout - a person who evaluates the talent of amateur athletes to determine if they would have success in the pros.

triple-double - an instance of a player scoring ten or more points, assists, and rebounds in one basketball game.

varsity - the main team that represents a school in athletic or other competition.

To learn more about Awesome Athletes, visit **booklinks.abdopublishing.com**. These links are routinely monitored and updated to provide the most current information available.

INDEX